The Pictures of Texas Monthly Twenty-Five Years

Rattlesnake Wrangler *by Jim Cammack*

SWEETWATER RATTLESNAKE ROUNDUP

"STATE OF THE ART" • APRIL 1992

Rancher Gil Stoner *by Andrew Yates*

STONER RANCH, UVALDE • *"HOME ON THE RANGE"* • OCTOBER 1996

The

INTRODUCTION BY STEPHEN HARRIGAN

Pictures of

EDITED BY D. J. STOUT AND NANCY MCMILLEN

Texas Monthly

GUEST CURATOR ANNE WILKES TUCKER

Twenty-Five

STEWART, TABORI & CHANG, NEW YORK

Years

Stanley Marsh 3, Eccentric *by Wyatt McSpadden*

CADILLAC RANCH, AMARILLO

"STATE OF THE ART" • SEPTEMBER 1990

Published in 1998 and distributed in the U.S. by Stewart, Tabori & Chang, a division of U.S. Media Holdings, Inc. 115 West 18th Street, New York, NY 10011

Distributed in Canada by General Publishing Company Ltd. 30 Lesmill Road Don Mills, Ontario, M3B 2T6, Canada

Distributed in Australia by Peribo Pty Ltd. 58 Beaumont Road Mount Kuring-gai, NSW 2080, Australia

Distributed in all other territories by Grantham Book Services Ltd. Isaac Newton Way, Alma Park Industrial Estate Grantham, Lincolnshire, NG31 9SD, England

Library of Congress Cataloging-in-Publication Data

Texas monthly : 25 years / by the editors of Texas Monthly.
  p. cm.
  Includes index.
    ISBN 1-55670-705-3 (hardcover)
    1. Texas—Pictorial works. 2. Texas—Biography—Pictorial works.
  I. Texas Monthly II. Texas monthly (Austin, Tex.)
  F387.T55   1998   97-28431
  976.4—dc21   CIP

Printed in Singapore

10 9 8 7 6 5 4 3 2 1

Book design by D. J. Stout
Design assistance and production by Nancy McMillen

Acknowledgments *The Pictures of Texas Monthly: Twenty-Five Years* was originally conceived by *Texas Monthly* art director D. J. Stout, who also designed the book and jacket.

Texas Monthly associate art director, Nancy McMillen, helped with the design and oversaw production. Her knowledge, experience, and organizational skills were priceless. Thanks also to Kathy Marcus and Hope Rodriguez of the *Texas Monthly* art department for their valuable assistance.

The magazine is indebted to Anne Wilkes Tucker, Gus and Lyndall Wortham Curator of Photography at the Museum of Fine Arts, Houston, who readily agreed to be guest curator for the book and exhibit. Her stellar reputation in the world of photography and her genuine enthusiasm for the photographs of *Texas Monthly* were important to this undertaking.

Texas Monthly custom publishing director, Cathy Casey, shepherded the book through publication. She managed a myriad of details with patience, grace, and charm. Cathy enlisted the help of Barbara Rodriguez, a literary agent and former staffer, who brought the book project to the attention of editor Linda Sunshine at Stewart, Tabori & Chang.

Stephen Harrigan, an accomplished novelist and screenwriter and a former *Texas Monthly* staff writer, wrote the thoughtful introduction. His past experience with the magazine, coupled with his sensitive powers of observation, made him the perfect choice. *Texas Monthly* senior editor Anne Dingus wrote the captions and additional text. Her tireless effort and good humor were much appreciated. Yet another former staffer, Jan McInroy, served as copy editor.

The magazine's public relations manager, Lisa Lawrence, has been an integral part of the *Texas Monthly* twenty-fifth anniversary project, which includes a special issue of the magazine and a traveling exhibition of the collection. Yvonne Anguiano provided assistance as well.

Finally, many thanks to *Texas Monthly* founder and publisher Michael R. Levy and editor Gregory Curtis, for their steady support and their belief in the importance of photography to the magazine.

Texas Monthly®

Foreword *by D. J. Stout*

WHAT DOES TEXAS LOOK LIKE? Well, to me, Texas looks like Danny Turner's portrait of a big-haired woman in a small-town beauty parlor, her wondrous coif like a shimmering pink planet in a solar system of hair dryers. Texas looks like Harry De Zitter's quiet rendering of a barbecue heaven, so comforting in its promise of eternal serenity. Texas looks like the impenetrable stare of actor Tommy Lee Jones, whose porous red face, tightly framed by Andrew Eccles in the warm evening light, becomes the gritty, weathered wall of a desert canyon. In the image of another face, this one captured by Mary Ellen Mark from the front seat of a police car, a woman apprehended in a drug-infested ghetto screams out with an expression so sorrowful and full of pain that her anguished wail almost rises up and out from the page. She, too, is what Texas looks like.

For twenty-five years, *Texas Monthly* magazine has been what Texas looks like. Since its first issue in 1973, every event, person, place, or thing of significance to the state has been chronicled, debated, analyzed, or praised between its covers. *Texas Monthly* has become an institution and a standard of excellence in publishing; its writing is heralded by a national audience. The same qualities that earned *Texas Monthly* admiration for its literary achievements have also given it an outstanding reputation for design, illustration, and especially photography. The magazine has published work from some of the most noted names in photography, including Richard Avedon, Annie Leibovitz, and James Balog. It has collaborated with renowned photographers like Helmut Newton, William Wegman, Mark Klett, Raymond Meier, and Dan Winters. *Texas Monthly* has long supported native talents, such as Beaumont's Keith Carter and Dallas' Geof Kern. The combination of this impressive list of contributors, the magazine's vast array of subject matter, and Texas' undeniable mystique evolved into a rich photographic record unparalleled by any other state.

The Pictures of Texas Monthly: Twenty-Five Years is a celebration of a remarkable visual heritage and a tribute to the photographers who have lent their considerable talent and vision to the magazine over the course of a quarter century. The 147 images in this collection have been chosen to represent the very best of that photographic legacy. Anne Wilkes Tucker, the highly regarded curator of photography at the Museum of Fine Arts, Houston, joined forces with *Texas Monthly*'s art directors, Nancy McMillen and myself, to make the choices for this book. In addition to choosing images based on photographic merit, we wanted the final selection to reflect the magazine's extensive roster of contributing photographers and its broad variety of subject matter. The cuts were difficult to make, and many great photographs were left on the table, but in the end, what began as a group of disparate images has come together in one impressive volume to become a complete picture of what Texas looks like.

Introduction *by Stephen Harrigan*

"YOU'VE GOT TO MAKE IT MYTHIC." During my years as a staff writer at *Texas Monthly*, that was the directive I heard most often from my editors. It didn't matter whether I was writing about a city council election in Dallas, a custody battle for a chimpanzee, or the purgatorial charms of the Chihuahuan Desert. What mattered was that finally the story be about more than itself, that it link up in some way with the magazine's theme, its great presiding question: Who do we Texans think we are, and who are we really?

From a writer's perspective, the photographs that make up this book seem strangely disembodied without the columns of prose that once accompanied them, and without the headlines, captions, and other typographical intrusions that once "explained" them. Disembodied, but not unmoored. I suspect that one of the main reasons these particular images were selected to represent the twenty-five years of *Texas Monthly*'s photographic legacy is that they are tethered to the myth as well, inspired by the idea that Texas is not just a region but a kind of vision. You sense the awareness and appraising intelligence behind these pictures. They are after something, just like the magazine's best writing has always been after something: some hitherto undiscovered element that will finally make possible a unified field theory of Texas.

The portrait of Texas that emerges in these pages is a formal one. With a few exceptions, the pictures are posed. The human subjects are usually looking straight at you, quite conscious of the figure they aim to cut, and even the animals are often depicted at a decorous remove from reality. The landscapes tend to be big and solemn and evocative, and the unpeopled interiors—a cafe, an empty movie theater—are studiously spectral. Another kind of magazine chronicling another kind of place might have filled a book with images that were more candid or casual, but the self-consciousness of these photographs strikes me as exactly the right strategy. What would be the point in trying to sneak up on Texas? The best way to chronicle such a storied and bombastic place is head-on.

These photographs take Texas on its own terms, but that doesn't mean they buy into the state's infamous blather about itself. The Texas that Richard Avedon implies in his portrait of a young snake butcher at the Sweetwater Rattlesnake Roundup is as spooky and soulless a place as can be imagined, and the glowering skinhead presented by Dan Winters seems to confirm the belief of certain prejudiced outlanders that our beloved state is a fount of troglodytic evil.

The Rio Grande *by Jim Bones*

Even allowing for such hyper-reality checks, the mood in this volume is rather celebratory—which is fitting, because that has always more or less been the mood of the magazine itself. I remember being surprised, when I saw the first issue of *Texas Monthly* in 1973, at how un-snide it was. At that time journalism was at a pitch of cynicism and mean-spiritedness, and it struck me as odd—steeped as I was in the callowness of the age—that the magazine seemed to regard Texas not as a target but as a subject. *Texas Monthly* didn't embrace all of the state's glorious hoo-hah, but it didn't dismiss it either. It was an insider's magazine, not in the sense that the people who produced it considered themselves distinct from and superior to the populace at large, but because they never pretended to have escaped the force field of the Texas myth.

When Mike Levy started *Texas Monthly,* he envisioned it as a writer's magazine, and that's pretty much what it is. (*Texas Monthly* has never had a staff photographer, though it customarily employs seven or eight full-time writers.) But over the years the magazine has made a profound visual statement, and nowhere more aggressively or unforgettably than in the photographs it has published.

To his considerable credit, Levy allowed the erection of a brick wall between his exuberantly opinionated self and the people he hired to actually produce the contents of the magazine. Though we gremlins in the editorial department could often hear the publisher throwing himself against that wall, he consistently honored the deal: The magazine was of him, but not by him. His enthusiasms, though, are hard to miss, and one of the most abiding is photography.

"When I started the magazine," he told me recently, "I always knew the critical component in addition to the writing would be photographs. The best graphic support for journalism is photography. Illustrations have their place, but they're certainly not integral or primary." I think Levy instinctively distrusts illustrations as potential breeding grounds for artifice and ambiguity, whereas a photograph by its nature has a certain baseline frankness that is more in keeping with his vision of what a magazine is supposed to impart.

But when I first saw these memorable photographs in *Texas Monthly,* they did not strike me as simple counterparts or graphic support for the articles, even when those articles were mine. Especially now, with their visual primacy secured between the covers of this book, the photographs make their own way and tell their own stories with ringing assurance. I once wrote a lengthy article about the Comanches, but when I look at Kurt Markus' portrait of a solitary Comanche man in ancestral dress gazing out into a canyon, his bare back to the camera and his morose posture hauntingly expressive, it is not immediately apparent to me what my thousands of words conveyed that this image doesn't. Although I remember Prudence Mackintosh's essay "The Soul of East Texas" as one of the finest pieces of writing to appear in the magazine, Keith Carter's glimpse of an East Texas mantelpiece crowded with family portraits nevertheless seems resoundingly complete and final without it. The same is true of James Evans' picture of a baby lying on a quilt in a room that is utterly barren except for a dozen stuffed animals hanging haphazardly from the walls. Who is this baby? What is the nature of the life she has been born into? Are the stuffed animals tokens of loving protection or of encroaching chaos? Turning to the April 1997 issue of *Texas Monthly*—in which this image appeared as part of a story by Robert Draper about the tiny Mexican border town of Boquillas—could tell us more, but there is also the possibility that we could learn too much. The striking thing about almost all the photographs in this book is how much of their power comes from mystery, from truths that are suggested but never quite revealed.

The subject matter is at times surprising—beetles, blueberries, a fiddling contortionist—but more often it is not. The icons of Texas are unabashedly catalogued herein, from the Rio Grande to Anna Nicole Smith. There are cheerleaders, Texas Rangers, beauty queens, craggy landforms, sheriffs, football players, savage racists, movie stars, preachers, coyotes, murderers, musicians, beauticians, cowgirls, politicians, billionaires, Aggies, birds in flight, and growling trigger-happy citizens of various persuasions. If you're from Texas, you know them all, but they have never before been captured with such conviction, intensity, and sly humor.

This book is a kind of core sample of Texas during the last quarter century, though to describe it as such makes it sound more scientific and deliberate than it really is. Like all such collections, its contents are something of an accident. But I doubt that a programmatic survey could have given us a truer account of our lives and preoccupations. Here we are: ornery, stalwart, show-offy, glamorous, deluded, principled, hateful, baleful, yearning, self-mocking, self-revering, reflective, triumphant, and—in the case of one bovine subject—slobbering.

What finally binds all of these images together is the remarkable creative cohesion of *Texas Monthly* itself. In the twenty-five years of its existence, this publication has had only two editors: Bill Broyles and Greg Curtis. They were friends in college, colleagues at the magazine since its first issue, and kindred spirits. What this has meant for *Texas Monthly* is a steadiness of vision and journalistic principle that has made the magazine one of the most respected in the country. The art directors who have worked under these two editors—Sybil Broyles, Jim Darilek, Fred Woodward, and D. J. Stout—have all had perceptibly different styles, but the visual evolution of *Texas Monthly* has always seemed to me to be harmonious and progressive, without the clanking shifts in fashion that prove so distracting in other magazines.

So this book is rightfully a testament to an institution, one that has become not just a chronicler but a vital component of Texas culture. The proof of that assertion is in the simple observation that without *Texas Monthly,* these wonderful photographs would not exist. And a world without Kent Barker's portrait of a ferocious country sheriff reclining with a poodle in his lap is not a place I would care to live.

Comanche *by Kurt Markus*

WICHITA MOUNTAINS, OKLAHOMA

"THE LOST TRIBE" • FEBRUARY 1989

Indian Pictographs *by Mark Klett*

‹ Rock Climber *by Laurence Parent*

HUECO TANKS STATE PARK, EL PASO COUNTY

"SOCIAL CLIMBERS" • NOVEMBER 1996

Shrimp Boat and Deckhand *by Raymond Meeks*

PALACIOS • *"A SHRIMP TALE"* • OCTOBER 1996

Environmentalist Tony Amos *by Rocky Kneten*

MUSTANG ISLAND • *"THE TEXAS TWENTY"* • SEPTEMBER 1996

Tire Dump *by Beryl Striewski*

HOUSTON • *"A DIRTY, ROTTEN MESS"* • FEBRUARY 1989

Ranch House *by Harry De Zitter* ›

Horton's Mantel *by Keith Carter*

WHARTON • *"THE SOUL OF EAST TEXAS"*

OCTOBER 1989

The Stampede Dance Hall *by Wyatt McSpadden*

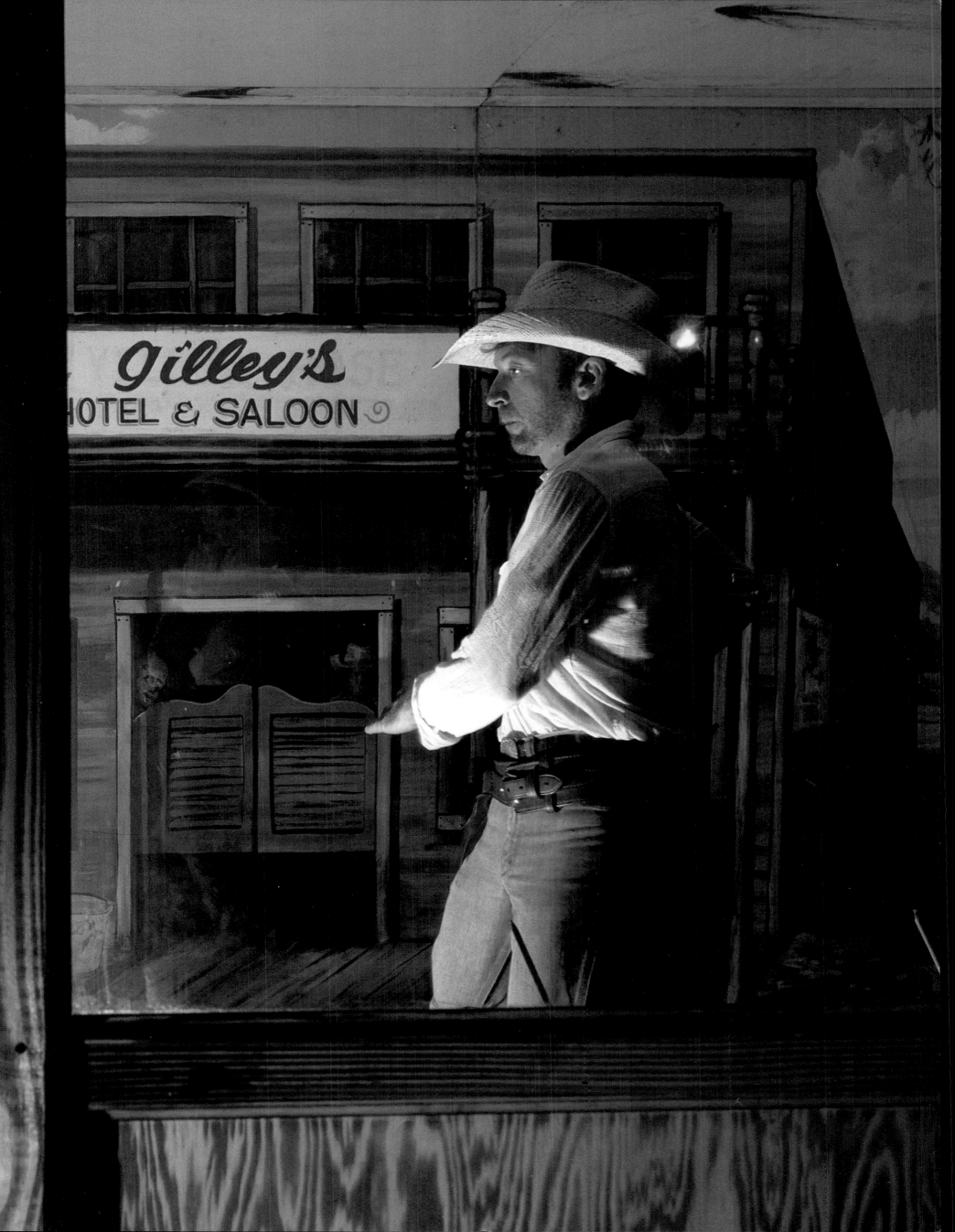

Louie Mueller's Barbecue *by Harry De Zitter*

Tommy Hill's Chat & Chew *by Birney Imes*

Blues Singer Miss Lavelle White *by Lee Crum*

HOUSTON • *"GOLDEN OLDIES"* • DECEMBER 1991

Texas Theater *by Dan Winters*

MCGREGOR • *"THE LAST PICTURE SHOWS"* • DECEMBER 1995

Actor Tommy Lee Jones *by Andrew Eccles*

ARKANSAS • *"THE FUGITIVE"* • OCTOBER 1993

Border Baby *by James H. Evans*

BOQUILLAS, MEXICO • *"THE CROSSING"* • APRIL 1997

Shoe Store *by Robert A. Widdicombe*

ISLA MUJERES, MEXICO • *"AMBIENT COLOR"* • APRIL 1985

Field Worker *by Geof Kern* ➤

PRESIDIO • *"NINETY MILES FROM NOWHERE"* • OCTOBER 1983

Cottonwood Borer and Tropical Ox Beetle *by Dan Winters*

AUSTIN • *"MEET THE BEETLES"* • JUNE 1992

Hooks Blueberries *by Tom Ryan*

DALLAS • *"CREAM OF THE CROPS"* • MAY 1993

Boy with Bee *by Keith Carter*

CATHEDRAL HIGH SCHOOL, EL PASO

"THE WAY OUT" • MAY 1990

Roadrunner in Flight *by Wyman Meinzer*

Bull Snake on a Sofa *by James H. Evans*

MARATHON • *"STATE OF THE ART"* • SEPTEMBER 1992

Trapped Coyote *by Wyman Meinzer*

KENDALL COUNTY • *"THE COYOTE WARS"* • JUNE 1981

Fay Ray in a Larry Mahan Boot *by William Wegman*

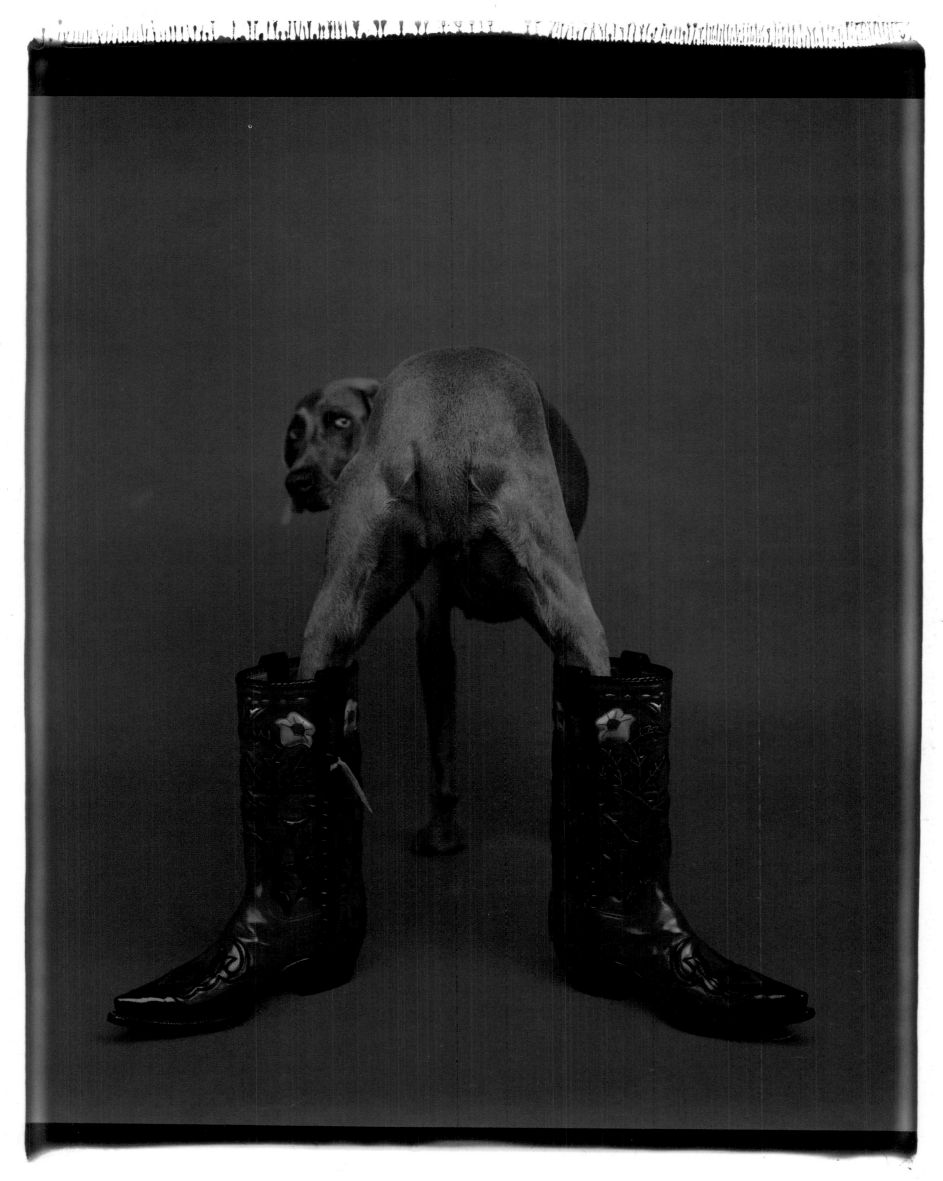

Fay Ray in Custom Boots *by William Wegman*

NEW YORK • *"GET ALONG, LITTLE DOGGIES"* • DECEMBER 1989

Clay Henry, the Beer-Drinking Goat *by Chip Simons*

Grand Championship Steer Auction *by Geoff Winningham*

HOUSTON LIVESTOCK SHOW AND RODEO • "*MY KIND OF TOWN*" • SEPTEMBER 1986

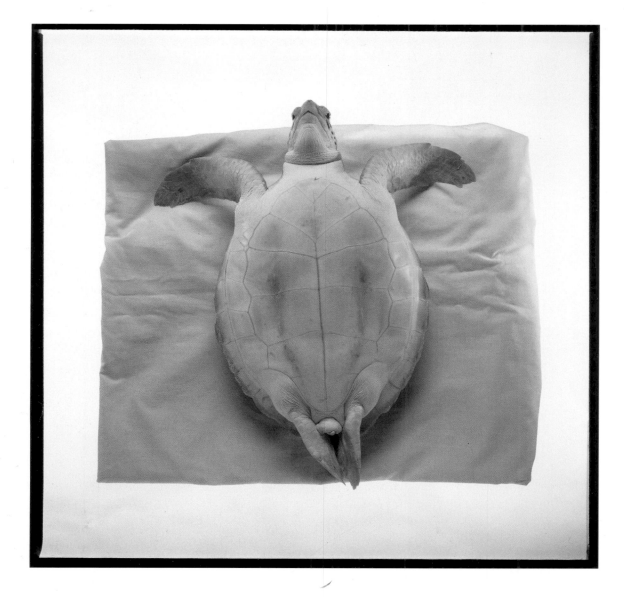

Atlantic Green Sea Turtle *by James Balog*

Musician Don Henley with Bald Eagle *by Laura Wilson*

Zydeco Musician Rockin' Dopsie *by Dennis Darling*

LAFAYETTE, LOUISIANA • "THE BIG SQUEEZY" • AUGUST 1988

Ragtime Pianist
The Grey Ghost *by Wyatt McSpadden*

AUSTIN • *"BLITHE SPIRIT"* • FEBRUARY 1989

Yogi Baird, the Texas Twister *by Brian Smale*

HOUSTON • *"ONE BRICK SHY OF A LOAD"* • OCTOBER 1988

Rock Band ZZ Top *by Michael O'Brien*

HUMBLE • *"HOW THEY DO IT"* • APRIL 1993

Tejano Singer Selena *by John Dyer*

CORPUS CHRISTI • *"THE TEXAS TWENTY"* • SEPTEMBER 1994

Singer-Songwriter Nanci Griffith *by Laura Wilson*

FRANKLIN, TENNESSEE • *"STATE OF THE ART"* • FEBRUARY 1995

Musician and Mystery Novelist Kinky Friedman *by Will van Overbeek*

KERRVILLE • *"LONG LIVE THE KINK"* • AUGUST 1988

Singer-Songwriter Willie Nelson *by Michael O'Brien*

AUSTIN • *"POOR WILLIE"* • MAY 1991

Children's Television Show Hosts
Don Mahoney and Jeanna Clare *by Jim Myers*

HOUSTON • *"OH, GIVE ME A HOME WHERE THE NAUGAHYDE ROAMS"* • OCTOBER 1987

Broadway Director and Choreographer Tommy Tune *by Andrew Eccles*

NEW YORK • *"HOW THEY DO IT"* • APRIL 1993

Film Director Richard Linklater *by Wyatt McSpadden*

AUSTIN • *"THE TEXAS TWENTY"* • SEPTEMBER 1995

Actress Sissy Spacek and Her Father *by Michael O'Brien*

QUITMAN • *"SISSY SPACEK'S LONG WALK HOME"* • FEBRUARY 1991

Actor Matthew McConaughey *by Dan Winters*

PALMDALE, CALIFORNIA • *"HIS TIME TO KILL"* • AUGUST 1996

Actor Lou Diamond Phillips *by Andrew Eccles*

NEW YORK • *"THE TEXAS TWENTY"* • SEPTEMBER 1996

Fitness Guru Susan Powter *by Greg Watermann*

DALLAS • *"THE SKINNY ON SUSAN POWTER"* • NOVEMBER 1993

Humorist Cactus Pryor *by Michael Patrick*

AUSTIN • *"SAY, HAVE YOU HEARD THE ONE*

ABOUT CACTUS PRYOR?" • AUGUST 1979

Writer Sarah Bird *by Mark Seliger*

AUSTIN • *"FUNNY BUSINESS"* • JULY 1990

Historian J. Evetts Haley *by Wyatt McSpadden*

Sarah Lea with Her Portrait by Husband Tom Lea *by Danny Turner*

EL PASO • *"A BRUSH WITH LIFE"* • MARCH 1989

Gatorfest Queen *by Michael O'Brien*

Border Debutantes *by Laura Wilson*

COLONIAL BALL, LAREDO • *"GOWN ON THE BORDER"* • MARCH 1995

Miss Universe, Chelsi Smith *by Andrew Eccles*

LOS ANGELES • *"THE TEXAS TWENTY"* • SEPTEMBER 1995

Model Anna Nicole Smith *by Andrew Eccles*

NEW YORK • *"THE MAKING OF A SEX SYMBOL, 1993"* • JULY 1993

Mary Kay Cosmetics Home Party *by Larry Fink*

DALLAS • *"HOSTILE MAKEOVER"* • NOVEMBER 1995

Cosmetics Tycoon Mary Kay Ash at Home *by Danny Turner*

DALLAS • *"THE TEXAS 100"* • AUGUST 1989

Chris Tiroff, *Lubbock*

Women with Big Hair *by Danny Turner*

"HOORAY FOR BIG HAIR!" • DECEMBER 1992

Jenny Glenn, *Childress*

Alexandria Trower, *Houston*

Mary Cheatham, *Corpus Christi*

Sharon Wilson, *Austin*

Western Wear *by Geoff Winningham*

Ten-Gallon Hat *by Raymond Meier*

Cowgirl Ann Holland Daugherty *by William Coupon*

GAGE HOLLAND RANCH, ALPINE

"IN PRAISE OF COWGIRLS" • NOVEMBER 1987

Young Lovers *by Max Aguilera-Hellweg*

Boy with Inner Tube *by Max Aguilera-Hellweg*

CIUDAD MIGUEL ALEMAN, MEXICO • *"FACES OF THE BORDER"* • MAY 1990

Former Mexican Revolutionary
Jesús González *by Dennis Darling*

BAYTOWN • *"COMPADRES DE LA REVOLUCION"* • NOVEMBER 1988

Kickapoo Indian Boys *by James H. Evans*

NACIMIENTO, MEXICO • *"THE FORGOTTEN PEOPLE"* • FEBRUARY 1997

Floating Woman *by M.K. Simqu*

DALLAS • "105°" • JULY 1985

Swimsuit Model *by Sally Gall*

CORPUS CHRISTI • "BATHING BEAUTY" • JUNE 1989

Beach Tourists *by George Krause*

Mardi Gras Parade *by Jim Cammack*

Spring Break *by Brian Smale*

SOUTH PADRE ISLAND • *"GIMME A BREAK"* • MAY 1992

Male Bonding *by Bill Kennedy*

SOMERVELL COUNTY • *"THE CALL OF THE WILDMAN"* • JANUARY 1990

Aggie Spirit *by Will van Overbeek* ›

TEXAS A&M UNIVERSITY, COLLEGE STATION

"BEING AN AGGIE IS NO JOKE" • JANUARY 1981

Injured Player at Pep Rally, *San Antonio*

Postgame Hero, *Taylor*

Friday Night Football *by Geoff Winningham*

"FOOTBALL HEROES" • SEPTEMBER 1979

Band Members, *Houston*

Drill Team, *Houston*

Kilgore Rangerette *by O. Rufus Lovett*

KILGORE • *"STATE OF THE ART"* • AUGUST 1990

Founder Gussie Nell Davis and the Kilgore Rangerettes *by Kent Barker*

KILGORE • *"GRANDE DAMES"* • APRIL 1990

Six-Man Football Team *by Laura Wilson*

MULLIN • *"TWELVE YARDS AND A CLOUD OF DUST"* • NOVEMBER 1995

Twin Cheerleaders *by Laura Wilson*

MULLIN • *"TWELVE YARDS AND A CLOUD OF DUST"* • NOVEMBER 1995

Dallas Cowboys Coach Jimmy Johnson *by James McGoon*

DALLAS • *"THE HUNGRIEST COACH"* • SEPTEMBER 1992

Football Great Earl Campbell *by Michael O'Brien*

BLANCO • *"HOW THEY DO IT"* • APRIL 1993

Houston Rocket Hakeem Olajuwon *by Arthur Meyerson*

HOUSTON • *"THE TEXAS TWENTY"* • SEPTEMBER 1994

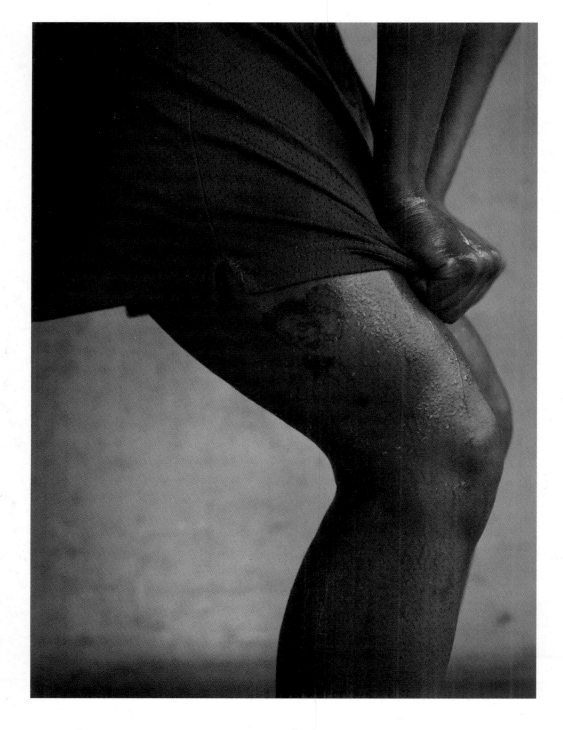

Lady Longhorn Cobi Kennedy *by John Huet*

THE UNIVERSITY OF TEXAS, AUSTIN

"A WHOLE NEW BALLGAME" • MARCH 1994

Heavyweight Champion
George Foreman *by Don Glentzer*

HOUSTON • *"HOW GEORGE FOREMAN*

FINALLY BEAT MUHAMMAD ALI" • SEPTEMBER 1989

Golf Legend Harvey Penick and
Writer Bud Shrake *by Michael O'Brien*

AUSTIN • *"THE OLD MAN AND THE TEE"* • DECEMBER 1993

The Tovar Brothers, Mexican Wrestlers *by Brian Smale*

SALTILLO, MEXICO • *"MASKED MARVELS OF MEXICO"* • AUGUST 1991

The Gonzales Brothers, Mexican Wrestlers *by Brian Smale*

RAMOS ARIZPE, MEXICO • *"MASKED MARVELS OF MEXICO"* • AUGUST 1991

Float Riders, *Leakey*

Cami Montgomery, *Seminole*

Quail Dobbs, *Big Spring*

Bree Worthington, *Big Spring*

Small-Town Rodeo *by Mary Ellen Mark*

"*R O D E O ,   T E X A S ,   U S A* " • M A R C H   1 9 9 2

Craig Scamardo and Cheyloh Mather, *Boerne*

The Cutler Family *by Keith Carter*

The Fernández Family *by Bruce Berman*

Trucker Couple *by Marc Wise*

Funeral Parlor Greeter *by Will van Overbeek*

BRADY • *"JUST THIS SIDE OF HEAVEN"* • NOVEMBER 1987

Stanley Marcus of Neiman Marcus *by Scogin Mayo* ➤

DALLAS • *"LIFE OF A SALESMAN"* • DECEMBER 1992

Heiress-Hotelier Caroline Hunt Schoellkopf *by Helmut Newton*

Socialite Lynn Sakowitz Wyatt *by Helmut Newton*

Oilman Oscar Wyatt *by Pam Francis*

HOUSTON • *"MEANER THAN A JUNKYARD DOG"* • APRIL 1991

Southwest Airlines CEO Herb Kelleher *by Mark Hanauer*

Billionaire Ross Perot *by Brian Smale*

DALLAS • *"POWER"* • DECEMBER 1987

Four Generations of Lloyd Bentsens *by Tomás Pantin*

HIDALGO COUNTY • *"FOR NAMES' SAKE"* • JUNE 1983

San Antonio Mayor Henry Cisneros and Son *by James McGoon*

SAN ANTONIO • *"CISNEROS AT FORTY"* • SEPTEMBER 1987

Environmental Enforcer John Hall *by Wyatt McSpadden*

AUSTIN • *"THE TEXAS TWENTY"* • SEPTEMBER 1994

Congressman Charlie Wilson *by David Barry*

Lady Bird Johnson, Former First Lady *by Michael O'Brien*

JOHNSON RANCH, STONEWALL • *"LADY BIRD LOOKS BACK"* • DECEMBER 1994

Lieutenant Governor Bob Bullock *by Wyatt McSpadden*

AUSTIN • *"THE TEXAS TWENTY"* • SEPTEMBER 1994

< Governor Ann Richards *by Annie Leibovitz*

AUSTIN • *"SADDER BUT WISER"* • APRIL 1994

Candidate George W. Bush *by Bob Daemmrich*

DICKINSON • *"STATE OF THE ART"* • OCTOBER 1994

Former President George Bush
And Millie *by Keith Carter*

The Reverend Dr. W. A. Criswell *by Greg Stephens*

DALLAS • *"THE POLITICS OF ARMAGEDDON"* • OCTOBER 1984

Father José Guadalupe Rodriguez *by Robert Maxham*

SAN ANTONIO • *"THE WEEK OF THE VIRGIN"* • DECEMBER 1985

Swami Prakashanand Saraswati *by Will van Overbeek* ‣

BARSANA DHAM, TRAVIS COUNTY • *"SWAMI DEAREST"* • OCTOBER 1995

Churchwomen *by Keith Carter*

CEDAR GROVE • *"THE SOUL OF EAST TEXAS"* • OCTOBER 1989

Tattooed Woman *by Dennis Darling*

ARLINGTON • "DESIGNS FOR LIVING" • JUNE 1989

Gutter Punk *by Jana Birchum*

Prostitute and Client *by Xavier Garza*

Arrested Drug Suspect *by Mary Ellen Mark*

DALLAS • *"THE WAR ZONE"* • NOVEMBER 1988

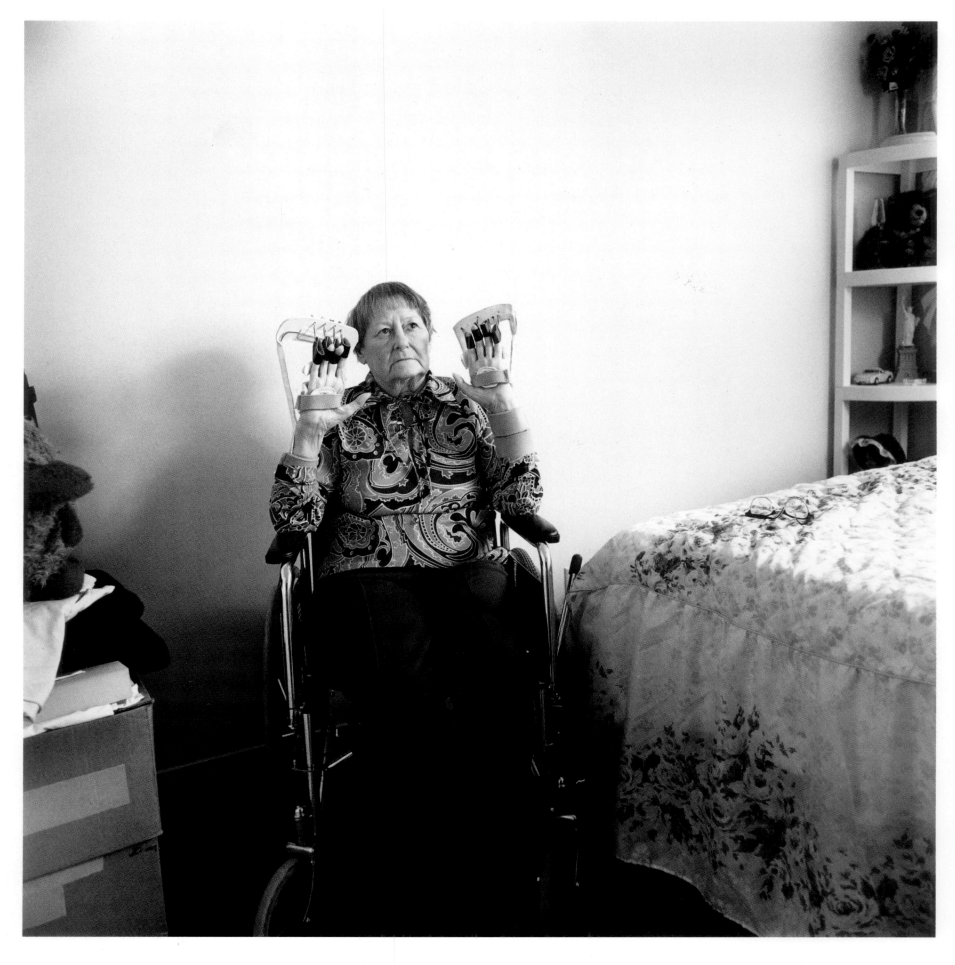

Arsenic Poisoning Victim *by Joseph Vento*

LLANO • *"POISONED WITH LOVE"* • MAY 1989

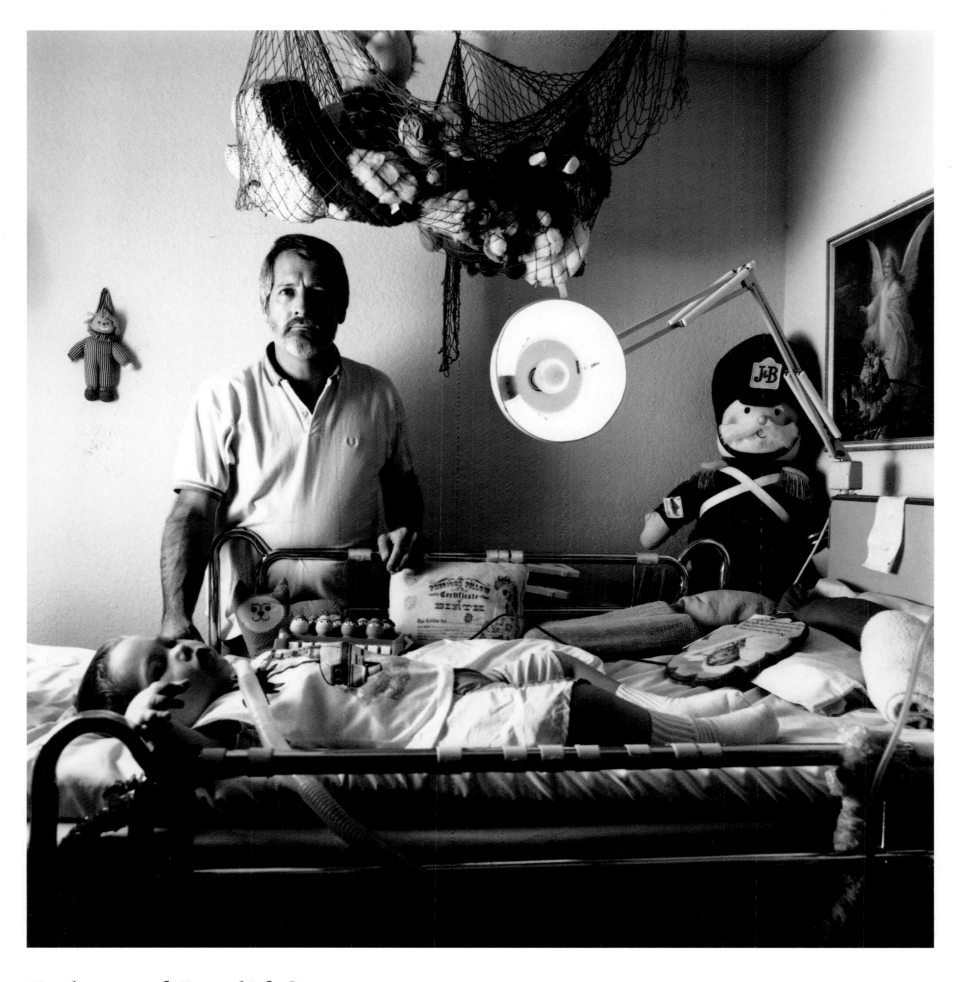

Father and Invalid Son *by Doug Milner*

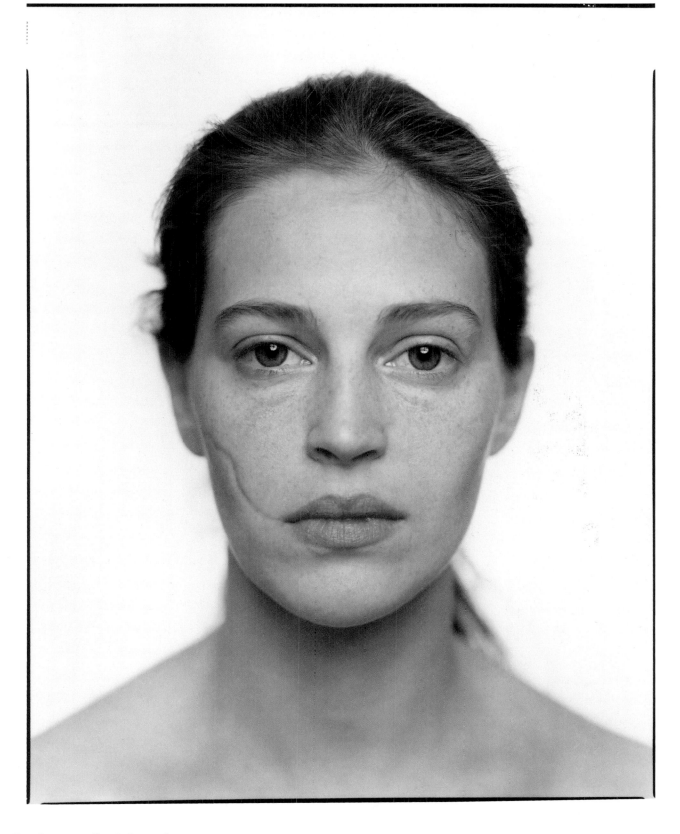

Model and Slashing Victim
Marla Hanson *by Michael Halsband*
NEW YORK • *"SCARRED"* • JANUARY 1993

Murder Suspects in Custody *by Stephen Shames* ›
HOUSTON • *"BLOOD IN THE STREETS"* • NOVEMBER 1991

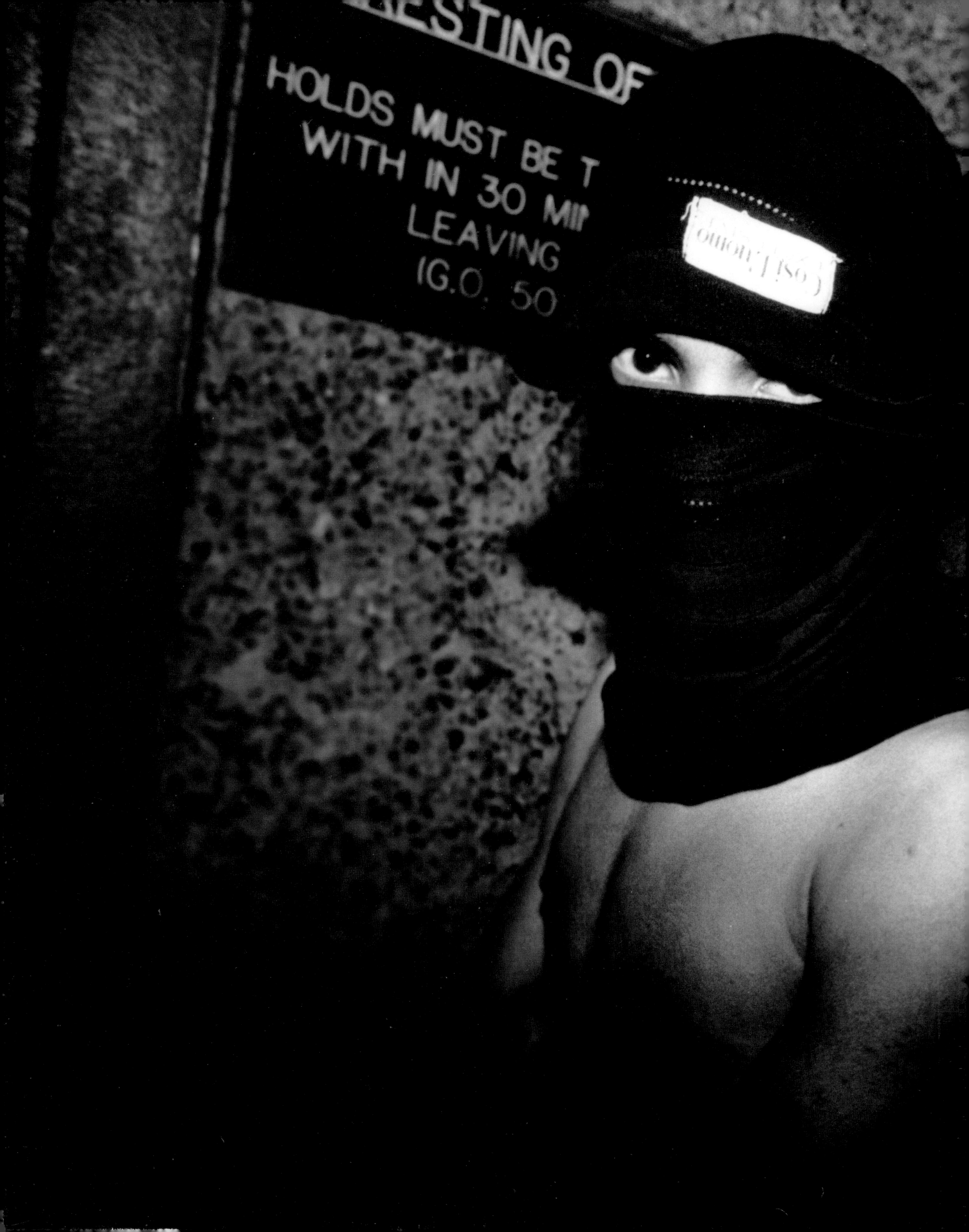
ESTING OF
HOLDS MUST BE T
WITH IN 30 MI
LEAVING
IG.O. 50

Boy with Shotgun *by Shelby Lee Adams*

Father and Son with Home Arsenal *by Robert Ziebell*

Black Militia Member and Grandmother *by Joseph Vento*

DALLAS • *"THE GHOSTS OF THE FREEDMEN"* • JULY 1991

Incarcerated Gang Member *by Dan Winters*

SAN ANTONIO • *"WE GET ALL HYPED UP.*
WE DO A DRIVE-BY'" • OCTOBER 1994

Nurse and Convicted Baby Killer
Genene Jones *by Robert Latorre*

GATESVILLE • *"THE DEATH SHIFT"* • AUGUST 1983

Inmate Cowboys *by Patrick Berry* ›

TEXAS PRISON RODEO, HUNTSVILLE

"STARS AND STRIPES" • FEBRUARY 1977

Texas Ranger Glenn Elliott *by Dan Winters*

Texas Ranger Joaquin Jackson *by Dan Winters*

ALPINE • *"THE TWILIGHT OF THE*

TEXAS RANGERS" • FEBRUARY 1994

Sheriff Rufe Jordan *by Kent Barker* ➤

GRAY COUNTY • *"HOWDY, SON, I'M THE LAW IN THIS COUNTY" • NOVEMBER 1984*

Self-Denial *by Geof Kern*

DALLAS • "THE NO DECADE" • JUNE 1987

The Photographers

Shelby Lee Adams follows in the tradition of Depression-era greats such as Walker Evans and Russell Lee. He has chronicled the mountain people of Kentucky for *Appalachian Portraits* (1993) and the upcoming *Of Time and Memory: Appalachian Photographs*. He lives in Salem, Massachusetts. *144*

Max Aguilera-Hellweg's photos have appeared in many publications, as well as in the movie *The Unbearable Lightness of Being*. The author of *The Sacred Heart: A Photographic Atlas of Invasive Surgery*, he now attends medical school in New York. *78, 79*

Richard Avedon is arguably America's greatest photographer. His career includes tenures as the chief fashion photographer for *Harper's Bazaar* and *Vogue*. He lives in New York. *160 (© 1985 Richard Avedon. All rights reserved.)*

James Balog's work for *National Geographic, Life, Smithsonian,* and other publications has taken him to the Arctic, the Himalayas, and other exotic locales. His books include *Wildlife Requiem* and *Survivors*. Balog lives in Boulder, Colorado. *44*

Kent Barker switched to photography after a knee injury forced him to give up a scholarship with the Joffrey Ballet. During his years in Dallas, he shot fashion assignments and magazine portraits. He now lives in Taos, New Mexico, where he specializes in landscape and travel photography. *92, 154*

David Barry has taken photographs for *Vanity Fair, W, Esquire, Interview, Spin, New York, Vogue,* and many other publications. He lives in New York. *121*

Bruce Berman's first assignment was documenting a sixties watershed, the 1968 Democratic National Convention in Chicago. Today he is known for his fine-art images of life on the U.S.-Mexican border. A resident of El Paso, he has also worked for editorial and commercial clients nationwide. *107*

Patrick Berry pursued freelance photography throughout the seventies and eighties for editorial, advertising, and corporate clients. His book *Lone Stars: A Celebration of Texas* focused on the Texas star as a design feature. He lives in Houston. *140, 150*

Jana Birchum, a former newspaper photographer, directed and produced *Wind Grass Song: The Voice of Our Grandmothers,* a film about the women who settled the Great Plains. Her photographs of social documentation have appeared in a variety of publications. She lives in Austin. *134*

Jim Bones, renowned for his landscape photography, also writes extensively about the North American wilderness. His work has appeared in *Audubon, Natural History,* and *Atlantic Monthly,* and his prints belong in museums nationwide. He lives in Marathon, Texas, where he works with the National Park Service on arid land restoration. *6*

Jim Cammack operated an East Texas studio devoted to commercial and editorial photography before signing on with the international agency Black Star in 1990. He currently lives in Bayfield, Colorado, where he divides his time between photography and training dogs. *1 (back cover), 85*

Keith Carter has published five monographs, including *Mojo* (1992); *Heaven of Animals* (1995); and *Bones* (1996). His work is included in the permanent collections of the George Eastman House, the Art Institute of Chicago, the Museum of Fine Arts, Houston, and more. He holds the Walles Chair of Art at Lamar University in Beaumont, his lifelong home. *20, 36, 106, 127, 132*

William Coupon has photographed Australian aborigines, African pygmies, Moroccan Berbers, Turkish Kurds, and other indigenous peoples. His photos have graced the covers of *Time* and *Newsweek,* as well as albums by Bette Midler, Wynton Marsalis, and Yo-Yo Ma. He lives in Santa Fe. *76*

Lee Crum, a New Orleans photographer, has worked on a variety of national advertising campaigns, including Nike and Wrangler. *27*

Bob Daemmrich of Austin has a strong news and editorial background. His sports photography includes coverage of the Summer Olympics in 1988, 1992, and 1996. He also takes studio and candid portraits. *126*

Dennis Darling notes that "with a name like Darling, you don't take pictures of flowers." A photographic specialty is subcultures, from motorcycle gangs to the Ku Klux Klan to the American Nazi Party. He is a journalism professor at the University of Texas in Austin. *46, 81, 133*

Harry De Zitter is a photographic purist whose images combine technical mastery and emotional vision. A native of Belgium, he is best known for his resonant American landscapes and interiors, which are informed and transformed by his European background. He lives in Chatham, Massachusetts, where he balances advertising and fine-art work. *18, 24*

John Dyer of San Antonio studied with Russell Lee, Garry Winogrand, and Geoff Winningham. He has taught photography and art at Trinity University, the University of Texas at San Antonio, and San Antonio College. His work includes series on conjunto musicians and boxers. *50*

Andrew Eccles of New York has photographed Demi Moore, Michelle Pfeiffer, John Travolta, and many other stars. He has worked for the likes of *Esquire, GQ, Time,* and *Life* as well as Warner Brothers, ABC, NBC, Sony, and Fox. Diverse other subjects include fashions by designer Geoffrey Beene (as worn by the New York City Ballet), the Zulu people of South Africa, and the *Exxon Valdez* oil spill. *28, 55, 60, 68, 69*

James H. Evans has documented the land and people of West Texas for a variety of national and international newspapers and magazines. He owns and operates the Evans Gallery in Marathon, Texas. *30, 39, 80*

Larry Fink is known for his inventive, influential documentary style. His books include *Social Graces,* a study of class distinctions, and *Boxing,* a visual essay on the sport. A professor of photography at Bard College, he lives in upstate New York. *71*

Pam Francis of Houston is an accomplished portraitist whose roster of clients includes numerous magazines and advertising agencies. "Getting to meet people is the best part of my job," she says. "Rich or poor, beautiful or hideous, remarkable or worthless, everyone I shoot is interesting to me." *114*

Sally Gall's fascination with water distinguishes her atmospheric photographs, such as those in her 1995 book, *The Water's Edge*. A resident of New York, she grew up in Houston. *83*

Xavier Garza's work has appeared in the *New York Times, U.S. News & World Report,* and the *Washington Post,* as well as many Texas publications. He was the personal photographer to former Texas Governor Mark White. He lives in Austin. *135*

Don Glentzer, an advertising and editorial photographer, lives in Houston. His clients include McCann Erickson, The Richards Group, Ogilvy & Mather, Weiden & Kennedy, *Entertainment Weekly,* and *Men's Health.* His "Historical Cemeteries" series is on permanent exhibit at the Texas State Cemetery in Austin. *101*

Michael Halsband documented the Rolling Stones' U.S. tour in 1981 and subsequently pursued fashion and editorial photography for *Interview, Art News, GQ, Vogue, Life, Self,* and other publications. A New Yorker, he is also a filmmaker and a director of music videos. *141*

Mark Hanauer started his career as a staff photographer for A&M Records in 1978. His work has appeared on numerous album covers as well as in *GQ, Newsweek, Vanity Fair,* the *New York Times Magazine,* and other publications. He lives in Los Angeles. *116*

John Huet of Boston is one of the nation's most prominent sports photographers. He has shot individual athletes from André Agassi to Jackie Joyner Kersee, as well as advertising campaigns for Reebok, Nike, Puma, Adidas, and other corporations. His latest book is *Soul of the Game. 98*

Birney Imes lives and works in Columbus, Mississippi. Completely self-taught, he is a fine-art photographer whose images have been collected in three books, *Juke Joint, Whispering Pines,* and *Partial to Home. 26*

Bill Kennedy of Austin juggles fine-art and commercial photography, portraiture, and location work. He also teaches photography at St. Edward's University and has coauthored a computer-interactive textbook on photography business education. *87*

Geof Kern opened his Dallas studio in 1979 and has since become internationally renowned for his work in magazines, advertising, and design. The recipient of a Grammy, a Cannes Palm d'Or, and a Cannes Gold Lion, he has produced numerous award-winning campaigns, including two for Matsuda and Neiman Marcus. *32, 77, 156*

Mark Klett, a veteran of dozens of solo and group shows, is known for his landscapes and urban vistas. He has authored eight books, and his prints are represented in some thirty collections. An associate professor at Arizona State University, he lives in Tempe. *11*

Rocky Kneten notes, "I arrived in Houston in 1984, just as the price of a barrel of oil approached the price of a milkshake. Looking back, I realize this wasn't so bad;

it gave me a lesson in hard work." Today his extensive roster of clients ranges from Baylor University to *Rolling Stone.* He also pursues landscape photography. *15*

George Krause addresses issues of religion, death, and sexuality in his fine-art images, which include street scenes in Mexico, Spain, Italy, and the United States, as well as tombstones and cemetery monuments, religious statuary, and nudes. A professor at the University of Houston, he has published several collections of his work. *84*

George Lange's images have appeared on the posters for *Liar, Liar, Chasing Amy,* and other films. He has contributed to *Esquire, New York, Vanity Fair,* and other magazines, and his commercial clients include GM, ABC, Disney, Paramount, Universal, and IBM. He lives in Santa Monica, California. *115*

Robert Latorre first worked as a photo stringer and a freelance photojournalist, crisscrossing South America, Europe, and the United States. Since 1975 he has lived in Dallas, where he specializes in commercial photography and commercial film production. *149*

Annie Leibovitz is one of the most prominent photographers of her generation. She is highly acclaimed for her celebrity portraits, many taken during her long associations with *Rolling Stone* and *Vanity Fair.* Her subjects have included John Lennon and Yoko Ono, Salvador Dali, Alice Cooper, Mick Jagger, Norman Mailer, and numerous other luminaries. She lives in New York. *124*

O. Rufus Lovett is a director of the Texas Photographic Society and a professor of photography at Kilgore College. Two of his longtime series subjects are the Kilgore Rangerettes and the town of Weeping Mary, Texas. He lives in Longview, Texas. *93*

Mary Ellen Mark, the author of eleven books, is internationally renowned for documentary photography, such as her photoessays on circuses and brothels in India and runaway children in Seattle. She has also produced the films *Streetwise* and *American Heart,* and works for a variety of corporations in the U.S. and abroad. She lives in New York. *104, 105, 136*

Kurt Markus terms his photographs "decidedly unslick." He has worked for *Rolling Stone, Vogue, Mirabella, The New Yorker, Men's Journal,* and *Harper's Bazaar,* as well as for advertising clients such as Nike, Sony, Armani, BMW, and AT&T. A resident of Kalispell, Montana, he has published two cowboy compendiums, *Barbed Wire* and *Buckaroo. 10*

Robert Maxham, a lifelong resident of San Antonio, worked as an advertising copy-

writer and creative director before turning to photography. His celebrity subjects have included Bob Hope, Sam Peckinpah, David Robinson, Kathy Ireland, and Selena. *129*

Scogin Mayo was introduced to photography by his father, a devoted amateur. He divides his time between commercial and editorial work for Neiman Marcus, Nordstrom's, Microsoft, Starbucks, Southwest Airlines, *Men's Journal,* and many other clients. He lives in Dallas. *110*

James McGoon says he "specializes in capturing the images of people." He has shot hundreds of pictures for dozens of magazines, from movie stars to HIV-positive children to politicians to ballet dancers. He lives in San Antonio. *97, 119*

Wyatt McSpadden is best known for his longtime chronicling of Cadillac Ranch, the automotive art installation outside Amarillo. He also handles editorial and commercial shoots for a variety of publications and corporations. A native of Amarillo, he lives in Austin. *4, 21, 47, 57, 64, 120, 122*

Raymond Meeks favors shooting in black and white and making his own prints. His fine-art images frequently take the form of environmental portraits or landscapes, often with people "to add scale or emotion." He lives in Columbus, Ohio. *14*

Raymond Meier has applied his distinctive still-life style to national print campaigns such as Calvin Klein; he has also adapted the signature Meier look to portraiture and fashion, notably for *Harper's Bazaar.* He lives in New York. *74*

Wyman Meinzer applied his bachelor's degree in wildlife management to a career in nature photography. His books include *Roadrunner* and *Coyote,* and his images have appeared in *Smithsonian, Audubon,* and other publications. He lives in Benjamin, Texas. *37, 38*

Arthur Meyerson handles corporate, advertising, and editorial work. His clients include Coca-Cola, Nike, Apple, *National Geographic,* United Airlines, American Express, and Motorola. He lives in Houston. *99*

Doug Milner of Poetry, Texas, was a veteran photojournalist best known for his stint at the *Dallas Times Herald.* In 1987 he became a freelance photographer for *Newsweek, Forbes, Fortune, Sports Illustrated,* and many other magazines. He died in 1996. Today his wife, Brenda, and daughter, Sophie Texanna, run Milner Stock Photography. *139*

Jim Myers notes that he "paid dues in L.A. after graduation—swept floors and was yelled at by self-important Hollywood photographers." He moved to Dallas in 1979, where he maintains a roster of print advertising clients and also pursues editorial work. *54*

Helmut Newton achieved international fame in the seventies while working primarily for French *Vogue*. His fashion shots are known for their distinctive combination of immediacy, controversy, and glamour. A native of Berlin, he lives in Monte Carlo. *112, 113*

Michael O'Brien first worked as a news photographer in Miami and later established a studio in New York. His commercial clients include GTE, Kodak, and Apple Computers, and his editorial work has appeared in *Life, National Geographic,* the *New York Times Magazine,* and other publications. He lives in Austin. *49, 52, 56, 66, 96, 100, 123*

Tomás Pantin, born in Caracas, Venezuela, moved to the United States in 1973 and obtained a photojournalism degree from the University of Texas. He concentrates on advertising and corporate photography in his Austin studio. *118*

Laurence Parent of Austin specializes in landscape, travel, and nature photography. His coffee-table book *Texas* appeared in 1995, followed in 1997 by *Official Guide to Texas State Parks.* He has worked for *Outside, Men's Journal, Newsweek,* and other publications. *12*

Michael Patrick pursued photography as a hobby for several years before he signed on as an assistant to various portrait and commercial photographers in Houston. In 1974 he moved to Austin—a decision that, he admits, was "based on proximity to lakes, not potential clients." Today he balances a variety of editorial and commercial assignments. *62*

Tom Ryan, a tabletop director and cinematographer, heads a division of Michael Schrom and Company, known for its studio close-up photography. His recent work has included commercials for United Airlines, Kraft, Taco Bell, 7-Eleven, and Tabasco. He lives in Chicago. *34*

Mark Seliger, a native of Houston, began working as a *Rolling Stone* photographer in 1987 and has since shot more than eighty covers. His books include *Crazy Sexy Cool,* a compilation of his portraits for *Us* magazine, and *When They Came to Take My Father: Voices of the Holocaust.* He has also directed music videos for Shawn Colvin, Hole, and other performers. He lives in New York. *63*

Stephen Shames is a freelance photojournalist and art photographer. In 1991 he published *Outside the Dream: Child Poverty in America;* three years later he created the nonprofit Outside the Dream Foundation,

which uses photography to publicize child-related crises and explore possible solutions. He lives in New York. *142*

Chip Simons is known for wide-angle photographs using colored strobes and light painting techniques. His "I Am a Dog" series ran in *Interview;* subsequent work has appeared on movie posters and album covers as well as in editorial spreads and print ads. He lives in rural New Mexico. *42*

M. K. Simqu's most recent photoessay focuses on alien plants threatening Florida waterways. Her work has appeared in a variety of magazines. She teaches at the Ringling School of Art and Design in Sarasota, Florida. *82*

Brian Smale has an extensive editorial clientele, including *Rolling Stone* and the *Washington Post Magazine.* Born and raised in Canada, he now lives in Brooklyn. *22, 48, 86, 102, 103, 117*

Greg Stephens of Dallas juggles fashion, beauty, and portrait photography. His commercial clientele includes Neiman Marcus, Mary Kay Cosmetics, and J.C. Penney, and his work has appeared in *Vogue, Harper's Bazaar, Allure, Seventeen.* and other magazines. *128*

Beryl Striewski specializes in black and white environmental portraiture and panorama photography. Her clients include Continental Airlines, Compaq Computers, and Houston's M. D. Anderson and Hermann hospitals. She lives in Houston. *16*

Danny Turner's work has been solicited by the likes of *Forbes, Outside, Sports Illustrated, Vanity Fair, Bon Appetit,* and *Entertainment Weekly,* and he also works for a diverse assortment of advertising clients. Many of his photographs, he notes, are in the permanent collection at his mother's house. He lives in Dallas. *65, 70, 72, 73*

Will van Overbeek's first major project was the book *Aggies: Life in the Corps of Cadets at Texas A&M.* He works on editorial assignments for *Time, Newsweek, Smithsonian,* and other publications, as well as doing commercial work for Nike, McDonald's, IBM, and other corporations. He lives in Austin. *53, 88, 109, 130*

Joseph Vento first worked as a contributing photographer for Andy Warhol's *Interview.* Subsequently his clients included major editorial and fashion names throughout Europe and the United States. Today he specializes in fine-art photography, dividing his time between New York and New Mexico. *138, 146*

Greg Watermann lives in Dallas, where he pursues portrait and fashion photography

for such publications as *Elle, Rolling Stone, Glamour, Cosmopolitan,* and *Mademoiselle.* His most memorable shoot was with Nirvana for the January 1992 cover shot of *Spin. 61*

William Wegman is famed for his whimsical shots of his pet Fay Ray and other weimaraners. His work has been exhibited and acquired by numerous national and international museums, and his honors and awards include two Guggenheim Fellowships. Among his books are *Man's Best Friend* and a variety of children's best-sellers. He lives in New York. *40, 41*

Robert A. Widdicombe, a former assistant to Eliot Porter, has taught college courses, designed books, and run his own advertising agency in addition to pursuing fine-art photography. He lives thirty miles south of Santa Fe, in a solar-powered house he built by hand. *31*

Laura Wilson's work has appeared in *The New Yorker,* the *New York Times Magazine,* the *London Sunday Times Magazine,* and other publications. She is the author of *Watt Matthews of Lambshead,* a photographic tribute to a legendary Texas rancher. She lives in Dallas. *45, 51, 67, 94, 95*

Geoff Winningham is a professor at Rice University in Houston. He has chronicled the classic Texas institutions of rodeo and high school football in *Going Texan* and *Rites of Fall.* His most recent volume, *In the Eye of the Sun,* focuses on Mexico's indigenous fiestas. *43, 75, 90, 91*

Dan Winters is known for celebrity portraits, photojournalism, and scientific photography. He has worked for *Rolling Stone, GQ, Vanity Fair,* and *Details,* as well as Nike, Sega, IBM, Paramount, and Warner Brothers. He also directs music videos and short films, including Sandra Bullock's *Making Sandwiches.* He lives in Hollywood. *29, 35, 58, 147, 148, 152, 153 (front cover)*

Marc Wise's best-known work documents life on the road for America's truckers. A truck driver himself, Wise has also taught photography in a variety of colleges. He lives in Brooklyn. *108*

Andrew Yates counts among his advertising clients Bank One, Pennzoil, Texas Lottery, Dell, and Southwestern Bell. In addition, he has supplied images for a variety of regional and national publications. He lives in Austin. *2*

Robert Ziebell arrived in Houston in 1983 as artist-in-residence at the city's Museum of Fine Arts. His work has been exhibited nationwide and has also appeared in numerous magazines. He has taught photography and film at the University of Houston and at Houston's Glassell School of Art. *145*

Boyd Fortin, Thirteen-Year-Old Rattlesnake Skinner *by Richard Avedon*